So Into Science!

EXPLORING THE NIGHT SKY

By Emmett Martin

Gareth Stevens PUBLISHING

Please visit our website, www.garethstevens.com. For a free color catalog of all our high-quality books, call toll free 1-800-542-2595 or fax 1-877-542-2596.

Library of Congress Cataloging-in-Publication Data

Names: Martin, Emmett, author.
Title: Exploring the night sky / Emmett Martin.
Description: New York : Gareth Stevens Publishing, [2019] | Series: So into science! | Includes index.
Identifiers: LCCN 2018013146| ISBN 9781538228876 (library bound) | ISBN 9781538232064 (pbk.) | ISBN 9781538232071 (6 pack)
Subjects: LCSH: Astronomy–Juvenile literature.
Classification: LCC QB46 .M37425 2019 | DDC 520–dc23
LC record available at https://lccn.loc.gov/2018013146

Published in 2019 by
Gareth Stevens Publishing
111 East 14th Street, Suite 349
New York, NY 10003

Editor: Therese Shea
Designer: Sarah Liddell

Photo credits: Cover, p. 1 vovan/Shutterstock.com; p. 5 Pozdeyev Vitaly/Shutterstock.com; pp. 7, 24 (telescope) Celig/Shutterstock.com; pp. 9, 24 (constellation) danmitchell/DigitalVision Vectors/Getty Images; p. 11 alexkoral/Shutterstock.com; p. 13 TuiPhotoEngineer/Shutterstock.com; p. 15 David Carillet/Shutterstock.com; p. 17 Matej Pavlansky/Shutterstock.com; p. 19 Terrence Emerson/Shutterstock.com; p. 21 janez volmajer/Shutterstock.com; p. 23 Alohaflaminggo/Shutterstock.com.

Printed in the United States of America

CPSIA compliance information: Batch #CW19GS: For further information contact Gareth Stevens, New York, New York at 1-800-542-2595.

Contents

It's night.
I see so many stars!

I can see more
with a telescope!

A constellation is
a group of stars.
This one is
the Great Bear!

I see a falling star!
It's not a star.
It's burning dust!

The moon looks like a circle.
It's a full moon!

The moon looks different sometimes. These are called phases.

The moon gets light from the sun.

I can see a planet.
It's Venus!

VENUS

Earth spins around
each day.
That's why we have
night and day!

I love the night sky!

Words to Know

constellation

telescope

Index